Our Country's Holidays

Martin Luther King Jr. Day

by Sheri Dean

Reading consultant: Susan Nations, M.Ed., author/literacy coach/ consultant in literacy development

Please visit our web site at: www.earlyliteracy.cc
For a free color catalog describing Weekly Reader® Early Learning Library's list of high-quality books, call 1-877-445-5824 (USA) or 1-800-387-3178 (Canada).
Weekly Reader® Early Learning Library's fax: (414) 336-0164.

Library of Congress Cataloging-In-Publication Data available upon request from publisher.
Fax (414) 336-0157 for the attention of the Publishing Records Department.

ISBN 0-8368-6506-5 (lib. bdg.)
ISBN 0-8368-6513-8 (softcover)

This edition first published in 2006 by
Weekly Reader® Early Learning Library
A Member of the WRC Media Family of Companies
330 West Olive Street, Suite 100
Milwaukee, WI 53212 USA

Managing editor: Valerie J. Weber
Art direction: Tammy West
Cover design and page layout: Kami Strunsee
Picture research: Cisley Celmer

Picture credits: Cover, © Francis Miller/Time & Life Pictures/Getty Images; pp. 5, 9, 15, 17, 21 © AP/Wide World Photos; p. 7 © Diana Walker/Time & Life Pictures/Getty Images; p. 11 © Robert W. Kelley/Time & Life Pictures/Getty Images; p. 13 © Delphine Fawundu/SuperStock; p. 19 © Vicky Kasala/The Image Bank/Getty Images

Printed in the United States of America

3 4 5 6 7 8 9 10 09 08 07 06

Note to Educators and Parents

Reading is such an exciting adventure for young children! They are beginning to integrate their oral language skills with written language. To encourage children along the path to early literacy, books must be colorful, engaging, and interesting; they should invite the young reader to explore both the print and the pictures.

In *Our Country's Holidays*, children learn how the holidays they celebrate in their families and communities are observed across our nation. Using lively photographs and simple prose, each title explores a different national holiday and explains why it is significant.

Each book is specially designed to support the young reader in the reading process. The familiar topics are appealing to young children and invite them to read – and reread – again and again. The full-color photographs and enhanced text further support the student during the reading process.

In addition to serving as wonderful picture books in schools, libraries, homes, and other places where children learn to love reading, these books are specifically intended to be read within an instructional guided reading group. This small group setting allows beginning readers to work with a fluent adult model as they make meaning from the text. After children develop fluency with the text and content, the book can be read independently. Children and adults alike will find these books supportive, engaging, and fun!

– Susan Nations, M.Ed., author, literacy coach,
and consultant in literacy development

Martin Luther King Jr. Day celebrates the life of Martin Luther King Jr. He worked hard to make sure everyone was treated the same.

In 1986, Congress said we should all celebrate King and his work on the third Monday in January. President Ronald Reagan signed papers making that day a holiday across the country.

When King was a boy, many white people thought they were better than black people. Sometimes they treated these African Americans badly.

OPEN
Come in
WHITE
ONLY
MAIDS IN WHITE UNIFORMS
PERMITTED

African Americans had to live in certain parts of town. They had to go to black schools. Some African Americans could not vote.

King had a dream. He wanted to change this. He wanted everyone to live, learn, and play together.

King spoke to many people about his dream. He led marches to show that people wanted to change.

ON THE MARCH
I AM
A

King did not believe in fighting. He did not believe hurting people would help his dream.

KEEP
THE
DREAM
ALIVE

King did change how people thought. He helped people to be treated the same.

On Martin Luther King Jr. Day, we learn about his life. We write about King and draw pictures. We give speeches about him. We think about how we can help people too.

MISSIONY BAPTIST

Glossary

African American – a person of African background who lives in the United States

Congress – the part of the government that makes laws

march – an event when people walk together to show their support for a goal

For More Information

Books

A Picture Book of Martin Luther King Jr. David Adler (Live Oak Media)

Martin Luther King Jr. Day. First Step Nonfiction (series). Robin Nelson. (Lerner Publications)

Martin Luther King, Jr. Day. True Books: Holidays (series). Dana Meachen Rau (Children's Press)

Martin's Big Words: The Life of Dr. Martin Luther King, Jr. Doreen Rappaport (Jump At the Sun)

Web Sites

Martin Luther King, Jr. Day
www.holidays.net/mlk
Hear King's most famous speech and learn about his life and the way we celebrate his work.

Index

About the Author

Sheri Dean is a school librarian in Milwaukee, Wisconsin. She was an elementary school teacher for fourteen years. She enjoys introducing books and information to curious children and adults.